The Attributes Of Lent

Dialogues About
Repentance, Sacrifice,
Humility, Commitment,
Faith And Service

MARTHA L. LEACH

CSS Publishing Company, Inc.
Lima, Ohio

Library of Congress Cataloging-in-Publication Data

Leach, Martha L., 1931-
  The attributes of Lent : repentance, sacrifice, commitment, humility, faith, and service / by Martha L. Leach
      p.   cm.
  ISBN 0-7880-0568-5 (pbk.)
  1. Lent. 2. Worship programs. 3. Dialogue sermons. I. Title.
BV85.L34   1996
242'.34—dc20   95-40437
                                                                          CIP

0-7880-0568-5   PRINTED IN U.S.A.

Dedicated to Pastor Stephen Kimpel for his encouragement, and to my husband Dwight, and my children, Laura and Ron Shreffler and David and Terese Leach, for their support of all my projects and for the love and joy of all my successes which they share with me.

This work is in memory of my son, Craig Leach, who died in an auto accident in 1991. His wonderful sense of humor and his zest for living were gifts he gave his family.

Table Of Contents

Repentance

Opening Hymn:
"Out Of The Depths I Cry To You"   Luther

Psalm 51:1-14 *(responsively)*

The Lesson

The Gospel: Luke 22:54-62

Dialogue: King David And Peter

Hymn: "I Lay My Sins On Jesus"

Offering

Prayer:
P: For hurtful things we've said,

C: Father, forgive us.

P: For thoughts which have festered and caused us distress,

C: Father, forgive us.

P: For wrongs done without thought or consideration of others' feelings,

C: Father, forgive us.

P: For feelings of envy and hatred,

C: Father, forgive us.

P: For lies and half-truths,

C: Father, forgive us.

P: For neglecting the needs of those near us and those far away,

C: **Father, forgive us.**

The Lord's Prayer

Benediction

Closing Hymn:
"Chief Of Sinners Though I Be"   McComb and Redhead

Repentance

Narrator: Tonight we will give some thought to the first of the attributes of Lent — repentance. Throughout the Scriptures, the prophets and others have reminded people about their sins and have encouraged repentance. It's a word which conjures up negative feelings because none of us likes to feel like sinful people, and **yet we are!**

Repentance begins with the acknowledgement that **we are indeed sinful.** Our guests from the scriptures tonight are David, King of Judah, and Peter, a disciple of Christ.

* * *

David: Hello! I did not see you sitting there. Are you alone?

Peter: Yes, I am quite alone — more alone than I've ever felt before.

David: My name is David. I'm on my way to Jerusalem. Would you care to walk along?

Peter: I am Peter. I would appreciate the company, but I want to stay away from the city today. Besides, the authorities may be looking for me. My Master has been arrested. I am so ashamed! When he needed my support the most, I let him down. I was so sure my faith was strong enough to see me through any trial, but I was wrong. Not once but *three* times I denied knowing him. How could I have done that?

David: Who is this "Master" you speak of?

Peter: He is Jesus of Nazareth. I have been a follower of his for nearly three years. I have seen him heal the lame, give sight to the blind, and show his love in a thousand ways. He even has power over the seas.

Once after great crowds had been following us for several days, Jesus climbed into a boat to get away — he needed to rest. We, too, got into the boat. Jesus fell asleep before we had pulled away from shore. When we were out on the water, the winds suddenly rose, and the waves were huge and pummeled our boat about. We were all sure we were going to drown. So we awakened Jesus. He stood up in the boat and rebuked the winds and the sea, and suddenly there was great calm. He questioned why we were afraid.

David: *(Excitedly)* Could he possibly be the Promised One, the Messiah?

Peter: There are times when I am sure he is the Son of God. And other times I have such doubts. In fact, one time he referred to me as "man of little faith."

It was the end of a very long day. The Master had been teaching the crowds who followed him, and once again we all felt a need to find a place to rest. He told us to get into a boat and go to the other side of the lake. He would come later, he said. When we were in the middle of the lake, again the winds came up, tossing the boat like a toy on the waves. It was very frightening, and all of us were drenched from the huge waves.

Suddenly a bright light shone across the water, and as it came closer, we could see the figure of a man. We were terrified! We thought we were seeing a ghost. Then when he spoke, we recognized his voice. "Don't be afraid," he said. "It is I." **He was walking across the water!** *(Pause)*

(Continues) I can be a prideful person at times, and I said, "Lord, if it is you, let me come to you on the water." He said, "Come." So I actually got out of the boat and walked toward Jesus on the water. What an exhilarating experience!

David: You actually walked on the water? I never had an experience like that. You're one up on me, Peter.

Peter: Well, the wind picked up, and I thought I could feel myself sinking. My faith abandoned me, and I screamed, "Lord, save me!" He reached out his hand and said, "O man of little faith, why did you doubt?" And we got into the boat.

I can see now that I am still a "man of little faith." I wonder what he's thinking of me tonight. How can he ever forgive me?

David: If he is the Son of God, he can and will forgive you. Take it from one who knows how God forgives.

Peter: I'm sure what you did was not nearly so sinful as denying my Master.

David: Oh, Peter, sin is sin, but if we're talking about degrees of sin, my sins top them all. You see, God had been my counsel and my guide since I was a child. He gave me so many gifts: music, writing, leadership, courage. He gave me so much courage that while I was still a young boy, I was able to fight Goliath, a man three times my size. And I was victorious with only a sling and a rock.

He enabled me to be a great military leader. He gave me protection countless times.

And God's prophet, Samuel, anointed me **King of Judah!**

11

Peter: You are David, the King of Judah?

David: Yes, Peter, I am he. And when you talk about the need for forgiveness, I can relate — for my sins were great!

I had everything a man could want — power, riches, beautiful wives, the love of my people — everything. Then I saw another beautiful woman, Bathsheba was her name, and I wanted her, too. But she already had a husband. Then she found she was going to have a child, and I worked desperately to cover my tracks. But sin breeds sin, and eventually, I sent the woman's husband into battle, encouraged the troops to withdraw, leaving him without support, and he was killed. I murdered the man as surely as if I plunged my sword into him.

That was a long time ago, but even now as it comes to mind, the pain of remorsefulness returns. *(Pause)*

(Continues) Bathsheba, the beautiful woman I wanted so much, became my wife after she mourned the loss of her husband. Our son was born soon thereafter, and we loved him very much. But it was through my friend, Nathan, a prophet, that I was made to realize the terrible wrong I had done.

Nathan told me of two men — one rich with many flocks and herds, and another very poor with only one lamb, which was treated like part of the family. The rich man had a guest, and not wanting to take a lamb from his own flocks, he took the poor man's only lamb, slaughtered it, and prepared it for his guest. Hearing this story made me very angry, and I asked Nathan to tell me who this dreadful man was, for he deserved to die.

Nathan said to me, "You are the man."

Then my sins came out of hiding, and I saw myself as God saw me — an adulterer, a thief, and a murderer. I fell on my knees and repented. Nathan assured me that God had forgiven me, but because of what I had done, our child would die, and I and my family would know much pain.

It all happened as he said. My house was plagued with trouble. But in the midst of this, I was reminded of a loving God who is also a just God. He gave Bathsheba and me another son, and we named him Solomon. He became the third King of Judah. And to him was given much wisdom, more wealth than anyone had ever known before, and the privilege of building the first temple for the Lord.

Peter: I've heard that story many times. And I also know that it was written, you were a "man after God's own heart."

I know I must repent. And you have affirmed that God is a forgiving God, and his Son surely must be also. Like you, I know now that I will be forgiven, but my denial will cost me a great price — perhaps even the life of the best friend I ever had.

David: Why do you say that?

Peter: Jesus told me only a few days ago that he would be crucified. We dined with him last evening, and he said that we would all fall away from him because of this night. And I very proudly declared, "They may all leave you, Lord, but I will never leave you." There was a great deal of sadness in his face when he looked at me. "Peter," he said, "you will deny me three times before the cock crows twice." And I said, "Even if I must die with you, I will not deny you." Those words will forever "ring" in my ears.

David: Don't you see? Repentance is the key to forgiveness. How blessed you are to have not only witnessed the Messiah but to have been one of his disciples. He chose you because he could see something in you that would prove valuable in his service. You are not through yet, Peter. I have a feeling God has a wondrous plan for your life, but his plan begins with your repentance. Then comes forgiveness. Take it from one who's been around and who has seen the love of God unfold in his life.

Peter: You were here at the right time, David. Your words were what I needed to hear. If you still want my company, I will walk back to the city. I must find out what they've done with my Master.

David: I will walk a ways with you, but I believe my task here is finished. I now know I'm leaving God's people in good hands.

* * *

Narrator: So having met and shared experiences of sin and repentance, the two friends have spanned the ages and learned from one another.

Sacrifice

Opening Hymn:
"Jesus, Refuge Of The Weary"   Wilde and Herrnhut

Psalm 51:15-19 *(responsively)*

The Lesson

The Gospel: Luke 2:41-51

Dialogue: Hannah and Mary, the Mother of Christ

Hymn: "Glory Be To Jesus"   Caswall and Filitz

Offering

Prayer:
   P: Thank you, Lord, for full and free salvation.

   C: May we forgive others as we are forgiven.

   P: For your example of caring and healing,

   C: May we be aware of the needs of others and willing to assist them.

   P: For your love of all people: black, white, Jew, Gentile, rich and poor;

   C: May we see others through your eyes, without discrimination.

   P: Thank you, Lord, for the sacrifice you made for us,

   C: May we be willing to tell others of your sacrifice and what it means to each of us.

15

The Lord's Prayer

Benediction

Closing Hymn:
"Alas! And Did My Savior Bleed"   Watts and Wilson

Lent 2 Dialogue
Hannah and Mary, the Mother of Christ

Sacrifice

Narrator: This week the second attribute of Lent — sacrifice — will be highlighted in the dialogue. There are many in the Scriptures who made sacrifices for God and his purposes. Two women — Hannah and Mary, the mother of Christ — are tonight's examples of sacrifice — each in her own way. The setting is a garden.

♦ ♦ ♦

(Mary is weeping. Hannah approaches.)

Hannah: Greetings! What a beautiful garden! My name is Hannah. May I come in? Oh! Why are you weeping?

Mary: Come in if you wish. I'm not very good company. My name is Mary. I have just returned from Golgotha. This garden belongs to my friend, John. He has asked me to stay with him now that . . . that my son is dead.

Hannah: You've lost your son? I am so sorry. I know you must be in great pain. Tell me what happened . . . was he ill?

Mary: Oh, no! He was a healthy, young man, just 33 years old — in the prime of his life. And he was **special.**

Hannah: How was he special, Mary?

Mary: My husband, Joseph, and I recognized that he was special from the day he was born. And I'll never forget when he was 12 years old. We took him to the temple in Jerusalem. When it was time to return to our home in Nazareth, Jesus was not with us, but we assumed he was in the crowd somewhere. After a day's journey when we stopped to rest for the night, we realized he was not with us.

Hannah: How worried you must have been!

Mary: Yes! Joseph and I returned to Jerusalem, and after much searching, we found him in the temple listening to the teachers and asking them questions. They were astounded that this boy was so knowledgeable about the Scriptures. When I scolded him, he reminded me that he must be about his Father's business. He was speaking of God, his father.

He dutifully went home with us. Joseph taught Jesus the carpenter's trade, but when he became 30, he told me he was called to preach to the hearts of the people and to do the work of his Heavenly Father. Joseph had died, and though we had other children, it was hard for me to give up my oldest son ... to see him leave his home.

Hannah: I know exactly how you felt. I, too, sacrificed a son to further the work of God's kingdom.

Mary: Tell me about your son, Hannah.

Hannah: I was married to a wonderful man, Elkanah. He had another wife also and she had several children. I had none. My husband was very kind to me even though I had given him no children. I must have caused him great distress because I would cry and I wouldn't eat. I don't know how he put up with me.

Mary: He must have loved you.

Hannah: Finally, one day when we had gone to Shiloh where Elkanah offered his yearly sacrifice, I went to the door of the temple. Weeping and praying, I made a vow that if the Lord would give me a male child, I would raise him to be a servant of the Lord.

Eli, the priest, saw me praying and asked what it was I was praying for so earnestly. I told him that if my prayer for a son was answered, I would bring him to the temple when he was weaned and leave him for Eli to train in the service of the Lord.

Mary: This is just like the story from the Scriptures. But how . . .?

Hannah: Yes, Mary, I truly am Hannah. I'm not sure why the Lord led me to this garden this evening. Maybe he felt I could help you through your grief somehow. You see, the Lord did bless Elkanah and me with a son. We called him Samuel, and just as I promised, when he was weaned I took him to the temple to live with Eli.

Mary: How did you find the courage to sacrifice your son for the Lord's service? It must have been very difficult to leave this small boy behind. Especially one you had waited and prayed for.

Hannah: The same way you gave up your son, Mary. We found our courage because we knew our sons must be about their Father's business. After Samuel had been with Eli for some time, one night he thought he heard Eli calling his name. He went to Eli to see how he could be of service, but Eli said he had not called him. Again, Samuel heard someone calling and went to Eli. Eli told him that he had not called. Eli realized that perhaps it was God who was calling Samuel. And he instructed Samuel to answer, "Speak, Lord, for your servant hears."

Sure enough, the voice called Samuel's name again, and Samuel responded, "Speak, Lord, for your servant hears." Can you imagine? God himself called Samuel to his service. Samuel became a great prophet and was given the honor of anointing the first two kings of Israel. If I had not been willing to give up my son, my people would not have had such a fine leader.

Continue with what you were telling me, Mary.

Mary: I knew Jesus was about his Father's business when we were invited to a wedding in Cana. I could see Jesus' life was totally directed by God. While we were at the wedding, they ran out of wine. I told them to ask Jesus for his help. He didn't disappoint us. He changed water into wine so the wedding festivities would continue without embarrassment to the host. But Jesus reminded me that the miracle was done to reveal the glory of God.

Hannah: How proud you must have been of your son.

Mary: Yes, I was. There were other miracles — miracles of healing and even raising some from the dead. But in addition to the miracles, Jesus offered forgiveness of sins to all those he touched.

Hannah: I can't believe what I'm hearing. Could your son, this Jesus, have been the Messiah, the promised one?

Mary: Some thought he was, but the things he said and did angered many, and today they **crucified** him because his teachings and his miracles frightened them. The government and religious leaders did not want the people listening to or following this man **who would not deny he was the Christ.** He had done nothing to deserve arrest, let alone the terrible death on a cross. It's like his pain is my own.

20

Hannah: No wonder you are suffering so. But if he is the Christ, the Messiah, then death cannot hold him. Have faith, Mary. You and I have sacrificed our sons for the service of the Lord, but think what Jesus has sacrificed for us and for his people. **He gave his life.**

(Mary turns her back; Hannah slips away.)

Mary: I know how he loved everyone — Jew, Gentile, children, men, women, and sinners. I can see that, even though his dying has caused me and his friends much pain, perhaps you are right. Death cannot hold him. Hannah, you've raised my spirits and given me hope. You came along just when I needed you. *(Looking around)* Hannah? Hannah? I don't know where you disappeared to, but thank you for sharing my grief and touching my life.

* * *

Narrator: So having met and shared experiences of sacrifice, these two women have spanned the ages and learned from one another. Many of us sacrifice or "give up" something during this special season. But we need to remember the sacrifices made by our Lord and Savior. By becoming human, he suffered and died that we might live.

Humility

Opening Hymn:
"Rock Of Ages, Cleft For Me" Toplady and Hastings

Isaiah 40:1-11 *(responsively)*

The Lesson

The Gospel: Luke 3:7-17

Dialogue: Moses and John the Baptist

Hymn: "Lord, Whose Love In Humble Service" Bayly

Offering

Prayer:

P: For the lesson of humility we learn from Moses, thank you, Lord.

C: Teach us to be humble.

P: For the example of unworthiness expressed by John the Baptist, thank you, Lord.

C: Teach us to spread the Gospel, putting the needs of others ahead of our own needs.

P: For our Savior's willingness to give up everything, including his life, for our forgiveness, thank you, Lord.

C: Teach us to sacrifice so that others will know of your forgiveness.

P: For all those who have given their time and abilities and, yes, even their lives, for sharing the "good news," thank you, Lord.

C: **Teach us to use our time and abilities in humble service.**

The Lord's Prayer

Benediction

Closing Hymn:
"God, Whose Almighty Word"   Marriott and de Giardini

Humility

Narrator: At one point in their career, the disciples asked Jesus, "Who is the greatest in the kingdom of heaven?" We suppose they were hoping Jesus' answer would be, "Why, you, of course. You who gave up everything to follow me."

Instead Jesus called to him a child and told the disciples, "Unless you turn and become like children, you will never enter the kingdom of heaven. Whoever humbles himself like this child, he is the greatest in the kingdom of heaven."

Humility is one of the most misunderstood qualities. Our best example is the Master himself. But tonight our character studies are of Moses and John the Baptist.

We find Moses along the Jordan River, where he has been observing John the Baptist teaching and baptizing believers.

* * *

Moses: Hello! I believe John is your name? I've been watching for a while. Your preaching is vibrant and stirring. Truly you have been given the gift of speech which reaches into the very heart and soul of those who listen.

John: I was given life so that I might prepare the hearts of the people for the Messiah. I was born to parents who were well beyond the age of having children. My mother, Elizabeth, always told me I was a gift from God. I'm not sure she still feels that way. I think she wonders about my way of life, my appearance, and the way I speak out against evil. Of course, I know she is concerned for my welfare, and well she might be.

Moses: What is the ceremony where you "dip" people into the river?

John: Once the people have repented of their sins, they are invited to be baptized. The "dipping" in the river is to remind them they are cleansed — their sins are washed away.

Moses: But some you turned away. I could not hear every word, but you sounded angry.

John: Oh! Those were some of the Pharisees and Sadducees, our so-called religious leaders. They know about repentance and forgiveness, and they, too, look for the "One who comes to save the world." But I cannot baptize them. They are self-righteous — their repentance is only on the surface. They need to feel remorse for their sins and turn from their prideful ways.

Moses: You certainly have been blessed with understanding and with the ability to express yourself. At one time, God asked me to be the spokesman for my people. But I felt I was not eloquent enough, and the words did not come easily. Of course, I was a man of many excuses. My people were held captive in Egypt. Their situation caused me pain, and I even murdered one of the Egyptians for mistreating them. But when God told me he had chosen me to lead my people out of Egypt, I gave all kinds of reasons why I could not.

John: Out of Egypt? Who are you?

26

Moses: I am Moses of the tribe of Levi. I was born at a time when my parents were in slavery. My mother plotted to save my life by setting me afloat in a basket near where the Pharaoh's daughter bathed. She found me and raised me in the luxury and security of the Pharaoh's palace. My own mother was my nurse during my early years.

John: Ah, Moses! I know your story well. You were the savior of the Israelites in those early years.

Moses: As I said, I was a man of excuses. I could not speak well. So God said Aaron, my brother, would speak for me. Then I said, "Who am I that I should go to the Pharaoh and tell him to release my people? The Pharaoh now thinks of me as a traitor." God said he would be with me. I went on to say that the Israelites would not believe me when I said God sent me. So God showed me miracles, such as turning a rod into a serpent and then back into a rod.

John: God has great patience with all of us.

Moses: God did get very angry with me. I must have been a terrible disappointment to him. But finally I did gather the courage to go to Pharaoh, and I discovered the works of God are wondrous. I led the Israelites for many years. Those were difficult, tumultuous times. They disobeyed God's commands many times, and I, too, was guilty of doing things my own way when I should have been listening to God. There were many times when he had to humble me and remind me that I was his unworthy servant.

John: Oh, but I remember reading in the sacred scrolls, "Now the man, Moses, was very humble, more than all men that were on the face of the earth."

Moses: You embarrass me! But I have always felt incapable of the tasks that God has given me. When you said I was the savior of the Israelites, that was not true. For everything was done as God commanded only by the wisdom and strength he provided for me. There is only one Savior and he is the one to come, the one promised by God.

John: He is already here, Moses. And I know what you mean by feeling unworthy to the task. For God's son, Jesus, the Promised One, is now teaching throughout the country. He came to me to be baptized or "dipped," as you say, several weeks ago. He was born to my mother's cousin, Mary, so he was no stranger to me. But I knew he was different. From an early age he was committed to his heavenly Father, and Moses, I, too, felt unworthy and most humble in his presence. I did not feel I should baptize him. He was righteous and without sin. But he insisted on the baptism to fulfill all righteousness.

Moses: You knew he was the Messiah?

John: I felt it in my heart. But then after he came up out of the water, the heavens opened and the Holy Spirit in the form of a dove alighted on him. And a voice from heaven was heard, "This is my beloved Son in whom I am well pleased." That clinched it. It was then I knew this man was the Promised One. I have heard he has not only taught about God's love to many but he also has healed many.

Moses: Are you going to continue to preach and baptize now that you've seen the Messiah?

John: I know I'm nearing the end of my life. It's only a matter of time before Herod arrests me and, yes, may even put me to death. I've been openly critical of Herod and his family, so I know my days are counted. But I have done what God put me here to do, so I am ready to die if I must.

28

Moses: You never know what God has planned for you. He is full of surprises. It seems death was never very far from me. I was saved from death shortly after my birth, as I told you. Then when I was about 40 years old, I saw an Egyptian beating one of my countrymen and anger took over. I killed the Egyptian and hid his body in the sand. Then I was afraid someone had seen me do that terrible deed so I ran into the hills and the pasture country of Midian. I was sure God himself would strike me dead, but he forgave me.

John: He still had a job for you to do, Moses.

Moses: You are right. And I already told you about all the excuses I made. But finally Aaron and I gathered courage to call on Pharaoh. God sent many afflictions on Pharaoh and his people, but he still would not give the Israelites their freedom. Finally, when God sent the angel of death and the firstborn of every family and flock were taken, Pharaoh gave in.

We were free at last. But Pharaoh quickly had a change of heart, and once again I felt death "hot on my heels." As we were approaching the Red Sea, Pharaoh's chariots and horsemen were bearing down on us.

John: I know the rest ... the waters parted, and you and all the Israelites safely reached the other shore. The waters then closed over the chariots and Pharaoh's soldiers, and they were drowned.

Moses: How good it is to know that those wonderful happenings have been handed down for generations! I led the Israelites through the wilderness for the next 40 years. But God was with us ... he provided us with food and our clothing never wore out. He gave us his law — written by his own hand on tablets of stone — not to make life more difficult for us but to make life easier.

John: Why did you not lead the people into the Promised Land?

Moses: I knew they were not ready physically or spiritually to move into the Promised Land. Their enemies were strong and well armed, and even though the years of hard work in Egypt had made them physically strong, they were no match for those who now occupied the land God gave them.

John: You never did see the land God promised his people . . . at least until now!

Moses: You are right, my young friend. Joshua took over and led the Israelites in their struggle to gain their land.

John: You knew what was best for your people, even though it meant you were "taking a back seat."

Moses: The same could be said for you, John. You've given your best for your people and you've prepared the way for someone greater than you.

John: We do have something in common don't we . . . most of all, the Messiah and the hope he brings.

Moses: Now that I know the Promised One has come, I can go in peace. Grace be with you, John!

John: And with you, Moses!

* * *

Narrator: Moses and John the Baptist — two people chosen by God to carry out his plans. Both were strong, yet humble, men, putting God first in their lives in spite of the consequences, known and unknown.

Commitment

Opening Hymn:
"Take My Life, That I May Be" Havergal and Havergal

Psalm 37:1-7 *(responsively)*

The Lesson

The Gospel: John 19:23-27

Dialogue: Ruth and John

Hymn: "Thy Life Was Given For Me"
Thy life was given for me.
Thy blood, O Lord, was shed
That I might ransomed be,
And quickened from the dead.
Thy life was giv'n for me;
What have I given for Thee?

Long years were spent for me
in weariness and woe,
That through eternity
Thy glory I might know.
Long years were spent for me;
Have I spent one for Thee?

O let my life be given,
My years for Thee be spent;
World fetters all be riv'n,
And joy with suff'ring blent.
Thou gav'st Thyself for me,
I give myself to Thee.

31

Offering

Prayer:
P: Thank you, Heavenly Father, for the Scriptures and the means by which they stir up within us a desire to serve you.

C: **Stir up within us a desire to give our time, talents, and treasure to serve you by serving others.**

P: For pastors, teachers, leaders in the church, and committed laypeople,

C: **Stir up within us a commitment to your service.**

P: For the blessing of worship and fellowship,

C: **Stir up within us a desire to be in your house at each appointed time.**

P: For the love of family, friends, and fellow Christians,

C: **Stir up within us a love for one another.**

P: For bountiful gifts of food, clothing, and other material blessings,

C: **Stir up within us a desire to share our many gifts.**

P: For Jesus Christ and his commitment to "die" that we might "live,"

C: **Stir up within us a thankfulness for Christ's life and death.**

The Lord's Prayer

Benediction

Closing Hymn:
"May We Your Precepts, Lord, Fulfill" Osler and Mason

Commitment

Narrator: Commitment is the attribute of this Holy Season which will be the focal point of this evening's worship. Someone once said, "God does not ask about our ability or our inability, but about our availability." Ruth and John are two personalities from the Scriptures who were available when God needed them and who were committed to the needs of those around them.

John is returning to his home after witnessing Jesus' crucifixion.

* * *

Ruth: Sir, I've been watching from a distance. My heart is heavy for you and for the woman whose son just died on that cross. Were you a friend of this man called Jesus?

John: Yes, he was the best friend I ever had. We worked very closely the last three years. I learned so much from him. He chose me to be one of his followers.

Ruth: I saw only you, his mother, and other women at the foot of the cross today. Where were the others?

John: I don't know. We were all fearful of what they might do to us. And I don't deserve any credit for being here today. Like the others, I deserted him when the authorities came to arrest him. Last night when we went into the garden with him, he asked us to watch and to pray. And we fell asleep! Three times he asked us to stay awake and be watchful. And we did not.

But this morning I had to be near him. I disappointed and deserted him last night, but today I had to be there. And I was glad that I was because he asked me to care for his mother. How awful if no one had been there to look after her.

Ruth: You truly are a man of commitment. I'm sure you have enough family of your own to care for. Good friend or no, that's a lot of responsibility.

John: It's the least I could do for my Master. His commitment is what we should be speaking of. Even with all his pain, his last thoughts were of his mother. He was the most selfless man I ever met.

Ruth: How did you meet him?

John: It was John the Baptist who introduced me to "the Lamb of God, who takes away the sin of the world." John bore witness to several of us. John was put into prison and eventually put to death, but not before he had prepared the hearts of the people for the message of the Messiah.

Ruth: Was Jesus really the Messiah?

John: I believe it with all my heart ... After John was imprisoned, I returned to my fishing business which I shared with my father, Zebedee, and my brother, James. Then one day Jesus appeared and told James and me to follow him. So we left the business in the hands of our father and the hired servants. That was a decision we never regretted. He taught us the true meaning of love, and we became close friends.

Ruth: From what I witnessed today, you were his only friend.

John: No, all his disciples loved him, except perhaps the one who betrayed him. Fear does strange things to people. I regret that I did not have the courage to stay with him last night. I owe him my life.

By the way, you didn't tell me your name. You seem very much interested in my friend, Jesus.

Ruth: I am indeed. You see, he's a distant relative of mine. I am Ruth, daughter-in-law of Naomi, wife of Boaz, and great-grandmother of King David.

John: You're Ruth? I can't believe it. Woman, you are a most wondrous example of commitment. I read in the Scriptures of your commitment to Naomi. If I remember correctly, you are a Moabite.

Ruth: You remember correctly! How exciting that you've heard of me. But it's as you said. Accompanying Naomi back to her home after the death of her husband and her two sons was the least I could do. Naomi had been so kind to me and to my sister, and she shared her faith in God with me. It changed my life.

When we returned to Bethlehem, Naomi's friends accepted me most graciously. Naomi had a wealthy relative who allowed me to glean in his fields so that we might have food to eat. Naomi then began scheming to have Boaz, the owner of the fields, take me for his wife.

John: From what I can determine, God had his hand in the plan also.

Ruth: I believe that to be true, for it was a wonderful marriage and God blessed us with a son. Our great-grandson was the second king of Israel. And Jesus, the one you call the Messiah, was born of the house and lineage of David. Tell me more about the Messiah.

John: There is so much to tell. He taught anyone who would listen. He loved and cared about all people. Jesus touched the eyes of a blind beggar by the name of Bartimaeus, and he was able to see for the first time in his life.

Thousands of people followed him to hear him teach and to be healed. I remember one time he was teaching in Capernaum. The house where he was teaching was filled with people. Suddenly, through an opening in the roof, a pallet was let down right in front of Jesus. A paralytic had been brought to Jesus for healing by four friends. Jesus told him his sins were forgiven, to rise up and walk. And the man did. Jesus not only healed, but he forgave their sins.

And Jesus loved children and always had time for them. Many times he would tell us and those he was teaching that we must have faith like a child.

Jesus was concerned about the everyday needs of the people, too. One time he was teaching a group of more than 5,000 people, and it was late in the day. Jesus told his disciples to find food for these people. We couldn't believe his request. How could we find food for 5,000 people? We had searched through the crowd and found five loaves and two fishes, but that would hardly feed one person. But then the strangest thing happened. Jesus took the five loaves and two fishes and blessed them, and suddenly there were baskets of bread and fish. We gave everyone something to eat and there were 12 baskets left over. We witnessed his power many times in many places, and yet each time we were astounded by what we saw. He truly was God in human form.

Ruth: What wonderful stories! John, you really should write a book. Future generations should read about this Jesus.

I, too, believe he was the Promised One. But if he is the Messiah, then how could they put him to death?

John: Oh, I don't think this is the end of our friend, Jesus. Last night before Jesus was arrested we ate together, and he told us many things. One thing stands out in my mind. He said, "A little while and you will not see me; and again, a little while and you will see me . . . because I go to the Father." I believe he had to take our sins to the cross to die with him so that we might have forgiveness and the hope of eternal life.

Ruth: I'm glad we met, John, and had a chance to get to know one another. Jesus was committed to dying so that we might have life — even those of us who died before he came. The commitments you and I have made are insignificant when compared to Jesus. But he expects us to continue to love, care, teach, and witness so all will know about his saving grace. Peace be with you, John!

John: Till we meet again!

*   *   *

Narrator: Two friends, spanning the ages, have shared the joy and hope of salvation through Jesus' death on the cross. Here are two people we can learn from and whose example we may follow.

Faith

Opening Hymn:
"I Am Trusting You, Lord Jesus"   Havergal and Baker

Psalm 105:1-11 *(responsively)*

The Lesson

The Gospel: Luke 23:39-49

Dialogue: Abraham and the Centurion

Hymn: "Were You There?"   Negro Spiritual

Offering

Prayer:
P: For the faith of Abel who offered acceptable sacrifices to God,

C: Thank you, Gracious Father.

P: For the faith of Enoch who was taken up so that he should not see death,

C: Thank you, Glorious Father.

P: For the faith of Noah, who followed instructions from God and built an ark,

C: Thank You, Heavenly Father.

P: For the faith of Abraham, who obeyed God even when it meant great sacrifice,

C: Thank you, Loving Father.

P: For the faith of Moses, who allowed God to use him to save his people,

C: **Thank you, Gracious Father.**

P: For the faith of the disciples, who left everything to follow Jesus,

C: **Thank you, Omnipotent Father.**

P: For the faith of the Centurion, who believed beyond all doubt,

C: **Thank you, Merciful Father.**

P: For Jesus, the Pioneer and Perfecter of our Faith,

C: **Thank you, Loving Father.**

P: Strengthen our faith through prayer, worship, and service,

C: **We pray in Jesus' name.**

The Lord's Prayer

Benediction

Closing Hymn:
"You Are The Way"   Doane and Edinburgh

Lent 5 Dialogue
Abraham and the Centurion

Faith

Narrator: Faith is the attribute of Lent which perhaps should have been considered before all others. For repentance, sacrifice, commitment, humility, and service are all the results of faith in our lives.

Tonight Abraham and the Centurion meet. As the Centurion returns to his tent and prepares to sleep, Abraham approaches.

* * *

Abraham: Greetings! It seems I've been walking for days. Do you have time for a weary traveler?

Centurion: I can see that you are very tired. Come into my tent. I've just checked out my troops and feel rather like a weary traveler myself. When we're on maneuvers, this tent is my home. It's not exactly a place to entertain visitors.

Abraham: I lived in a tent all my life. My wife, Sarah, and I traveled a great deal, and tents were our home. Our son, Isaac, was born in a tent. We knew no other home.

Centurion: Where do you come from? Where is your home?

Abraham: My first home was in Ur of the Chaldeans ... then Haran, Shechem, Bethel, and Hebron. God kept me on the move.

Centurion: God? Your God?

Abraham: I always believed there was but one God. When my wife and I lived in Ur, there were idolators all around us. My father, my wife, and I moved from Ur to Haran. While in Haran, my father died, and it was then God told me to move from there to a land he had promised me. He said he would make of me a great nation and my name would be great.

Centurion: You mean you left your country and relatives and traveled without knowing where you were going? What faith!

Abraham: When God calls, I listen! He has blessed me and my family many times in many ways. But my faith was not always what it should be. Many years ago, God told me he would make me the father of a multitude of nations.

I didn't understand. One has to have children to be the father of a multitude of nations. Sarah and I were both over 90 years old ... well past the age to have children.

Some years before, Sarah and I had been impatient for children of our own, and Sarah thought I should take Hagar, her maid, for my wife also. I did and Hagar had a son. After that there was much strife between Hagar and Sarah. Further, God told me that the promises of a great nation would not stem from Ishmael's birth, although his descendants would be many also.

Centurion: I know something of your God. Are you Abraham, the father of the Israelites?

Abraham: I am he. How is it that you, a Roman soldier, would know about me?

Centurion: When I was a boy, I had a good friend who was one of the Jews. I was intrigued by the faith of his family, and they inspired me with their hope in the future . . . They're expecting a savior, the Messiah. I was fascinated by the wonderful stories my friend's family had passed down for generations. My Roman friends called them "crazy" and referred to them as the "fanatics." But I knew there was something to this faith. You could see it in their eyes . . . in their daily lives. But go on with what you were telling me.

Abraham: As I said, God promised Sarah and me many descendants. In fact, he sent three messengers to tell me that Sarah was going to have a son. Sarah overheard, and she could not suppress her laughter, for we were both old.

But Sarah did bear a son and we named him Isaac, which means laughter.

But my faith was to be tested again. When Isaac was still quite small, God said I must take him to Moriah and offer him as a burnt offering on one of the mountains. I could not believe God would give me a son after so many years and then ask me to sacrifice him. But my faith told me I must do as he asked.

My heart was heavy, and Isaac kept asking questions like, "Where is the lamb for the burnt offering?" Never has anything been so difficult for me.

I had prepared the wood, tied my son to the wood on the altar, and raised my knife to slay him, when God spoke. He said now he could see that I feared him, and I was to take Isaac down from the altar. There in the thicket was a ram God had provided for my sacrifice. What a prayer of thanksgiving I offered that day!

God always kept his promises down through the ages. The only one he has yet to keep is the promise of a savior.

Centurion: Oh, Abraham, I believe your God has kept that supreme promise also. You see, there is this Jesus of Nazareth who is a teacher and a healer. He gathers crowds wherever he goes. His message is one of love. I've observed him healing the sick, giving sight to the blind, and making the lame walk.

It was not so long ago near my home in Capernaum that I met him face to face. My servant was terribly ill — paralyzed even . . . and I was distressed over his suffering. I had heard the Teacher was in the area, and when I found him, I asked him to heal my servant. Jesus said he would come to my home and heal him. But I felt my home wasn't worthy to such an important visitor. I begged him just to "say the word" and my servant would be healed. He looked at me in astonishment, and he said, "Not even in Israel have I found such faith."

I didn't think of it as faith. Something inside me said he could heal my servant. Jesus said, "Go; be it done for you as you have believed." And my servant was healed!

Abraham: Do you know where this Jesus is? Take me to him.

Centurion: I wish I knew if he were still alive. Last week the soldiers in my charge and I were given the duty to guard this Jesus. He was arrested, interrogated, and beaten just because he said he was able to destroy the temple of God and rebuild it in three days. And when they asked him if he was the King of the Jews, he would not deny it.

It broke my heart to watch. I kept thinking perhaps he could escape or do one of his miracles, but he went bravely to his death. He was crucified. And when he had drawn his last breath, there was much noise and an earthquake as though God were giving us a sign. And my soldiers and I agreed, "Truly this was the Son of God."

Abraham: God once again provided a lamb to be sacrificed for us, just as he promised. But if he is the Son of God, death will not deter him.

Centurion: That's the interesting part of the story. Some of my soldiers were guarding Jesus' tomb and **his body disappeared!** The soldiers told me his disciples stole his body. I couldn't prove it, but it was rumored that the soldiers had taken a bribe and that the man, Jesus, was alive and had been seen in several places.

I believe he lives! I cannot believe otherwise.

Abraham: Yours is a great faith! We must keep the faith and trust that God keeps his promises. *(Pause)* I feel rested now, even exhilarated! Thank you for sharing your tent and your faith.

* * *

Narrator: Two men of faith meet and share experiences. It doesn't matter that they lived at different times — only that they shared a faith and a love for God's son. The conversation between these two men should serve to show us that God expects us to share with all people our faith, our love, and our material blessings.

Service

Opening Hymn:
"As Saints Of Old"   Christierson and Sateren

Psalm 116:12-19 *(responsively)*

The Lesson

The Gospel: John 12:1-8

Dialogue: Rahab and Mary of Bethany

Hymn:
"O Master, Let Me Walk With You"   Gladden and Smith

Offering

Prayer:
   P: Thank you, Heavenly Father, for the many examples of service in your Holy Word.

   C: For the service of Deborah and Gideon to their people in times of strife.

   P: Thank you for those who give simple, quiet service.

   C: For Martha who cared and provided comfort for our Lord and for Mary who listened.

   P: For those whose service was a beacon in the life and death of our Lord,

   C: For the woman who anointed Jesus with expensive oils and for Joseph of Arimathea who gave up one of his family's tombs.

P: For those whose service is different and pronounced,

C: For Elijah and his demonstration of God's power over Baal.

P: For those who provide safety and well-being for your people,

C: For Rahab who granted protection to the Israelite spies.

P: For those who provide food and clothing for the poor,

C: For Elisha's gift of meal and oil for the widow and for Dorcas' generous gift of clothing to those in need.

P: Thank you, Heavenly Father, for those who gave spiritual service.

C: For the prophets and for Peter, Paul, Stephen, and others who sacrificed so the Gospel could be shared.

P: For all those today who provide service of all kinds, in all ways, great and small,

C: Thank you, Lord, and instill in us a desire to show our faith by giving service wherever needed.

P: Above all else, we thank you for the service of your Son, Jesus Christ, whose gift of salvation is full and free and in whose name we pray ...

The Lord's Prayer

Benediction

Closing Hymn:
"In Christ There Is No East Or West"   Oxenham

Service

Narrator: Tonight Rahab, the Canaanite, meets Mary of Bethany. Their means of "service" were quite different, but each served in her own way.

Each of us has some way or ways we share our faith through service. In his description of the last judgment, the Master said the righteous will ask, "When did we see you hungry and feed you or thirsty and give you drink? And when did we see you as a stranger and welcome you or naked and give you clothing? And when did we see you sick and in prison and visit you?"

"And the king will answer them, 'I say to you, as you did it to the least of these, my brothers, you did it to me.' "

Let's listen in as Rahab and Mary meet at the well in Bethany where Mary has come to draw water.

* * *

Mary: Greetings! I am Mary. You must be a stranger in our village. I've not seen you before.

Rahab: Yes, my name is Rahab. May I have a cup of water? It seems like I've been walking for days, and it is hot and dusty on the road.

Mary: Certainly. Where have you come from?

Rahab: My home is in Jericho. I am a Canaanite.

Mary: It's been many years since anyone has referred to themselves as Canaanites. I see you are dressed somewhat differently than I or my neighbor women. What did you say your name was?

Rahab: I am Rahab. Before I came to know the God of the Israelites, I was a priestess of the Canaanites.

Mary: There was a Rahab who lived many years ago. She was used by God to save the Israelite spies before the fall of old Jericho. Today she is one of our heroes of faith. *(Hesitates)* You couldn't possibly be that Rahab.

Rahab: I am one and the same. I'm not sure about being a "hero of faith," however.

Mary: Oh, Rahab, yours was a great service. God uses all kinds of people with all levels of faith. But he accomplishes the work of his kingdom through the faith and service of his people. Come, let's sit in the shade. *(Excitedly)* Please, give me a first-hand account of the spies, the scarlet cord, everything.

Rahab: You've heard even of the scarlet cord? Well, Mary, I gained much because of what you call my service. My family and I were given our lives. But let me start at the beginning.
　　Jericho was an evil, heathen city. As I told you, I was a priestess of the Canaanites. My family and I had a very nice home right on the walls of the city of Jericho.

We had heard how the God of Israel dried up the water of the Red Sea before Moses and the others when they came out of Egypt. We also knew what happened to the Amorites and to kings Sihon and Og. We lost our courage and became fearful. I believed that your God was the one true God, and when the Israelite spies came to my door, I knew God had sent them. The king of Jericho had heard about the spies and sent messengers saying the spies were to be handed over to the king. I lied to the king's messengers and said the men left by way of the gate after it was dark. I had hid the men under stalks of flax on the roof of our house. The king's men went out of the city to search for them. Then I helped the spies out of the window and down the wall by rope.

Mary: Rahab, not only did you do a great deed, but you showed great courage.

Rahab: I'm not sure it was courage, because I made the men promise they would save my life and the lives of my family when Jericho was destroyed. The men told me to bind the scarlet cord in the window, and when they came to take Jericho, they would save everyone in my household.

I did as they told me. And a few weeks later when Joshua and his soldiers surrounded the city and the walls of the city fell, the soldiers came and took me and my household out of the city. Every other person and animal in the city was destroyed. My family alone was saved. We gave thanks and praise to your God.

Mary: What a wonderful story of faith and service!

Rahab: I did only what I felt compelled to do, for I could see the gods of my people were powerless. Yours is the one true God.

Mary: And, I believe, you are an ancestor of Jesus Christ, the Messiah. The scrolls tell us you are the mother of Boaz

51

and the grandmother of King David. The Messiah is of the house and lineage of David.

Rahab: I don't understand, Mary. You mean the Messiah has come?

Mary: Oh, yes. And he visited in my home quite often. My sister, Martha, and brother, Lazarus, were also close friends of his. He thought of our home as his — a place to recuperate from his busy and often stressful way of life. Even when he visited he would tell us of God's promises, and we were enthralled with his stories. I loved to listen as he spoke of life hereafter and the work that remained for all of us to do. I never tired of listening to him. Lazarus, too, was intrigued by his humility and the love which he displayed — not only in words but in the many miracles he performed, the healing and comfort he gave.

Rahab: Mary, tell me more of what he was like. What kind of miracles did you witness? To listen is serving also. Since you listened so intently, you can now share his words and acts with me.

Mary: Jesus, that's what we called him, said that listening was **the good part** of what is expected of us. You see, my sister was distraught with me because I spent so much time with the Master and left her to do the work. Jesus explained that listening is an important factor in the life of one who follows Christ.

But you see, Martha was "serving" also. She's been criticized so often for "doing" instead of listening. But both of us came to realize that faith, the listening part, and work, the doing part, are both important and necessary.

Rahab: Oh, I agree. But tell me of the Messiah's miracles.

Mary: We heard about his many healings, but there was only one miracle which I witnessed. My brother, Lazarus, had taken ill and, in spite of everything we did, he became worse. We decided to send for Jesus since we had heard he was in Jerusalem. But the messenger returned without Jesus. Martha was disappointed, but I felt the Master must have good reason, even though his good friend lay close to death.

(Sadly) Our brother died and together Martha and I prepared his body for burial. Our hearts were broken because we would miss him terribly. We both knew that he would rise again on the last day — the Master told us many times that death was not the end of all things — that there would be life eternal for believers.

Then about four days after we buried Lazarus, Jesus came to Bethany. Martha went to meet him and then returned for me. Jesus told us that He was the Resurrection and the Life, and those who believed would not die.

Then he asked where Lazarus was buried, and we showed him the way to the tomb. Many of our neighbors accompanied us. When we got there, Jesus said a prayer and then told some of the men to roll the stone away from the tomb. What was he planning to do? We all looked at one another, wondering.

Then Jesus called out, "Lazarus, come forth!" And he did — Lazarus came walking out of the tomb. He was alive and well! The Master said, "Unbind him and let him go." Can you believe it? Lazarus was dead, and now he was alive!

Rahab: Mary, are you sure it was not just some terrible trick?

Mary: If I hadn't seen it, I probably wouldn't have believed. But Lazarus was dead and now he is alive. We heard that some wanted to kill both Jesus and Lazarus because of this miracle.

(Hesitating) They did kill our friend, Jesus. They crucified him because they were afraid of him and afraid the people would overthrow the rulers and make him king. It was horrible what they did to him, and my family and I felt great pain at losing our good friend.

Rahab: How could he be the Messiah, if they were able to kill him?

Mary: There's more to the story. It was a painful experience for us, but Martha's faith came shining through. She kept reminding us that Jesus said He was the Resurrection and the Life.

Then on the first day of the week after Jesus was crucified, some women had gone to his tomb with their spices. When they got there, his body was not there. But an angel was there, and the angel said, "He is not here. He is risen!"

Can you imagine our joy on hearing that he had risen from the dead? Death could not hold him. He paid us a brief visit soon thereafter. He indicated he was going away, but this time he was going to be with his Father, and he would be preparing a place for us. He will come again and take us with him. He left us with that great hope.

Rahab: Mary, this is the greatest news of all. The Messiah has come and he has conquered death.

Mary: He left a command for us, too. To have faith in him and his promise is most important, but he made it clear that we have a job to do. We must continue to serve by witnessing to all humankind and by feeding both body and soul of our neighbors both near and far away.

In your heart, Rahab, you knew how best to serve your God and you did it with great courage and faith.

Rahab: I can now see that service is a result of faith — faith in action. I must be on my way. I've truly enjoyed our visit. My soul is at peace knowing that the Messiah has come.

* * *

Narrator: These two women lived ages apart, but both depict a faith which resulted in two kinds of service. We read in 1 Peter 4:10, "As each has received a gift, employ it for one another, as good stewards of God's varied grace." Rahab and Mary of Bethany were both willing servants and good stewards of "God's varied grace."